WELCOME TO THE GUIDE FOR *HUMAN* NINTH EDITION!

This handy guide links *Human Exceptionality* to Houghton Mifflin's *Video Cases in Education* in a variety of ways. In addition, this Guide will provide linkages between the Video Cases and the PRAXIS II Teacher Preparation exam.

GUIDE CONTENTS

Publisher: *Patricia Coryell*
Sponsoring Editor: *Shani Fisher*
Senior Marketing Manager: *Amy Whitaker*
Development Editor: *Julia Giannotti*
Editorial Assistant: *Jill Clark*
Marketing Assistant: *Samantha Abrams*
Senior Art and Design Coordinator: *Jill Haber*
New Title Project Manager: *Susan Peltier*

Printed in the U.S.A.

ISBN 10: 0-547-04650-2
ISBN 13: 978-0-547-04650-1

123456789–VHO–11 10 09 08 07

I. AN INTRODUCTION TO *HOUGHTON MIFFLIN VIDEO CASES* FROM THE AUTHORS

Dear Students and Professors,

Welcome to the Teaching in Action Media Guide that accompanies *Human Exceptionality—School, Community, and Family*, Ninth Edition! The main purpose of this Guide is to directly connect our textbook with *HM Video Cases*—an exclusive, award-winning, new multimedia series published by Houghton Mifflin.

As you will see, each Video Case is 4–6 minutes long and provides an inside look at real classrooms, teachers, and students from diverse settings. Each Video Case is quite compelling in its own way.

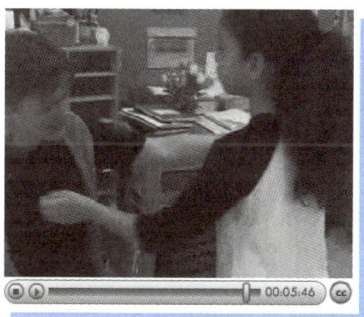

This Guide links the individual Video Cases with specific chapters and pieces of content from our text. Through the Video Cases, educational theories and strategies will be brought to life right before your very eyes!

In addition, these Video Cases provide a shared "field experience" for the entire class. All students can observe the same classrooms, teachers, and children in action. This shared observation provides excellent opportunities for class discussion, homework assignments, and group work!

Enjoy the Video Cases and please visit our text website **college.hmco.com/PIC/hardman9e** for more information!

Sincerely,

Michael Hardman, Clifford Drew, and M. Winston Egan

The next few pages will walk you through an actual Video Case and its various accompanying features.

1) Opening Screen

Below is the opening screen. This screen will appear every time you open a Video Case. You will access the main Video Case from this screen.

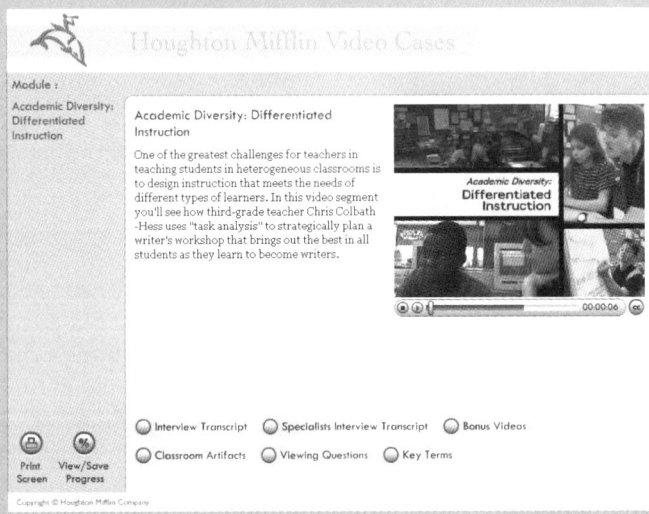

To view the Video Case, click on the **play** arrow underneath the black screen. At the very bottom of the page, you will see different buttons that will lead you to additional components of the Video Case—interview transcripts from the teachers, bonus video clips, classroom artifacts, student viewing questions, and key terms.

2) *Interview Transcripts*

For each Video Case, several different teachers (and other school professionals) were interviewed and asked to speak about the case topic. The results of these informative interviews are part of each Video Case. Just click on the **Interview Transcripts** button and you will have access to these valuable transcripts.

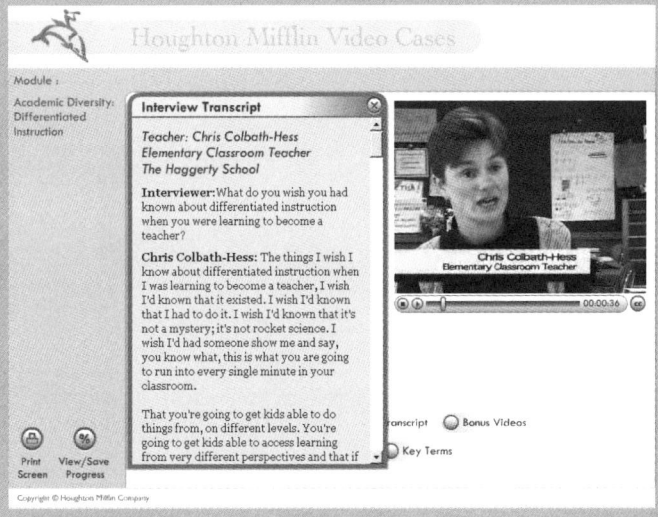

3) *Bonus Videos*

The screen below shows the **Bonus Videos** feature.
Each Video Case includes several bonus clips. These are
additional pieces of footage from the Video Case that
extend the action and story within the Video Case.

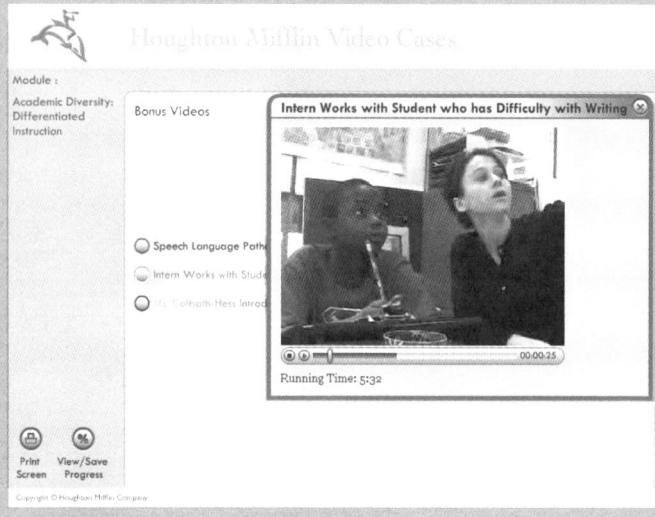

4)   *Classroom Artifacts*

The screen below provides an example of the **Classroom Artifacts** feature. This feature allows students and professors to view actual classroom materials from the Video Case—such as the teacher's lesson plan, worksheets used in the lesson, bulletin board materials pertinent to the case, or sample student work.

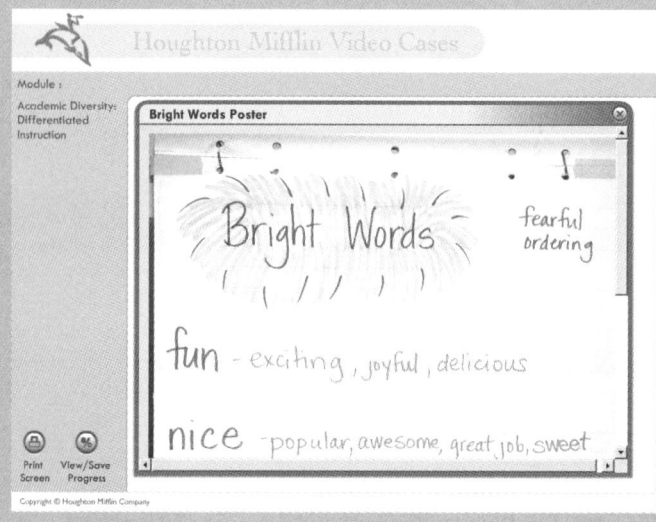

5) *Viewing Questions*

The screen below shows the **Viewing Questions** feature. These are reflective questions that professors can assign for homework, projects, or group work. In addition, the Video Case interface allows students to e-mail their answers directly to their instructor.

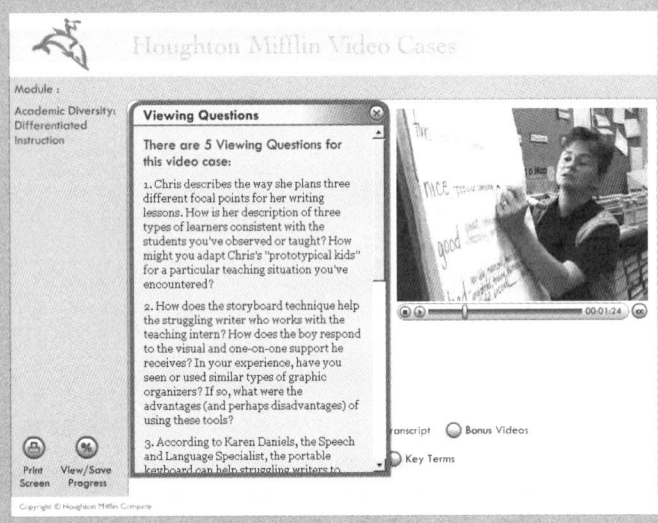

6) *Key Terms*

Several cases have a button for **Key Terms.** This button is present if a case contains a key concept or term. Click on this button and the terms and definitions for the case will appear in a pop-up window.

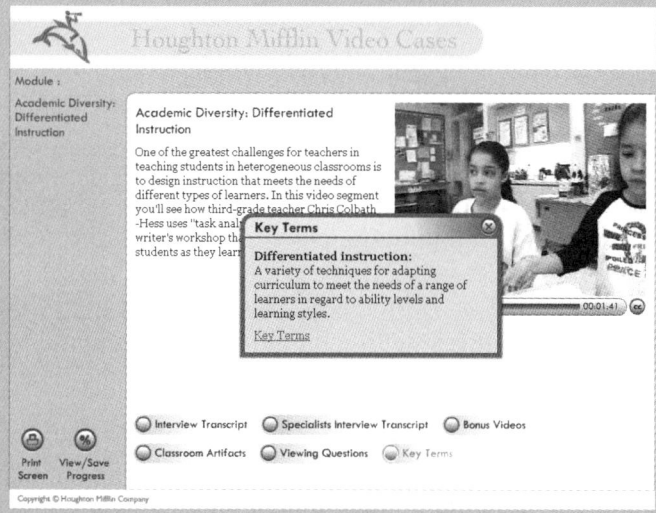

MATCH THE VIDEO CASES TO KEY CONCEPTS IN YOUR TEXT

This grid matches the various HM Video Cases to specific chapters and concepts within **Human Exceptionality**.

Chapter in Hardman, *Human Exceptionality*, 9/e	Matching HM Video Case	Exact Page Reference in the Text
Chapter 1: Understanding Exceptionality	Teaching as a Profession: Collaboration with Colleagues	16–19
Chapter 2: Education for All	Foundations: Meeting the Demands of Educational Legislation	27–32; 41–44
Chapter 2: Education for All	Students with Special Needs: The Referral and Evaluation Process	32–35
Chapter 2: Education for All	Teacher Accountability: A Student Teacher's Perspective	41–44
Chapter 3: Inclusion and Multidisciplinary Collaboration in the Early Childhood and Elementary School Years	Inclusion: Classroom Implications for the General and Special Educator	74–76
Chapter 3: Inclusion and Multidisciplinary Collaboration in the Early Childhood and Elementary School Years	Inclusion: Grouping Strategies for Inclusive Classrooms	76–78
Chapter 4: Transition and Adult Life	Developing Student Self-Esteem: Peer Editing Process	96
Chapter 5: Multicultural and Diversity Issues	Diversity: Teaching in a Multiethnic Classroom	114–115
Chapter 5: Multicultural and Diversity Issues	Culturally Responsive Teaching: A Multicultural Lesson for Elementary Students	114–115
Chapter 5: Multicultural and Diversity Issues	Bilingual Education: An Elementary Two-Way Immersion Program	121–122
Chapter 6: Exceptionality and the Family	Home-School Communication: The Parent-Teacher Conference	151
Chapter 6: Exceptionality and the Family	Communicating with Parents: Tips and Strategies for Future Teachers	151

Table continued on next page . . .

Chapter in Hardman, *Human Exceptionality*, 9/e	Matching HM Video Case	Exact Page Reference in the Text
Chapter 7: Learning Disabilities	Elementary Reading Instruction: A Balanced Literacy Program	186–189
Chapter 7: Learning Disabilities	Inclusion: Classroom Implications for the General and Special Educator	196
Chapter 8: Attention-Deficit/ Hyperactivity Disorder	Including Students with High Incidence Disabilities: Strategies for Success	215
Chapter 8: Attention-Deficit/ Hyperactivity Disorder	Classroom Management: Best Practices	220
Chapter 8: Attention-Deficit/ Hyperactivity Disorder	Metacognition: Helping Students Become Strategic Learners	221
Chapter 9: Emotional/ Behavioral Disorders	Classroom Management: Handling a Student with Behavior Problems	249
Chapter 9: Emotional/ Behavioral Disorders	Elementary Classroom Management: Basic Strategies	253–255
Chapter 9: Emotional/ Behavioral Disorders	Social and Emotional Development: Understanding Adolescents	256
Chapter 10: Intellectual Disabilities	Assistive Technology in the Inclusive Classroom: Best Practices	281
Chapter 10: Intellectual Disabilities	Inclusion: Grouping Strategies for Inclusive Classrooms	287
Chapter 11: Communication Disorders	Assistive Technology in the Inclusive Classroom: Best Practices	304
Chapter 12: Severe and Multiple Disabilities	Foundations: Meeting the Demands of Educational Legislation	329–330
Chapter 13: Autism Spectrum Disorder	Including Students with High Incidence Disabilities: Strategies for Success	359
Chapter 13: Autism Spectrum Disorder	Classroom Management: Best Practices	361–362
Chapter 14: Traumatic and Acquired Brain Injury	Classroom Management: Best Practices	382

Table continued on next page . . .

Chapter in Hardman, *Human Exceptionality*, 9/e	Matching HM Video Case	Exact Page Reference in the Text
Chapter 15: Hearing Loss	Teaching Technology Skills: An Elementary School Lesson on PowerPoint	411
Chapter 15: Hearing Loss	Expanding the Definition of Literacy: Meaningful Ways to Use Technology	411
Chapter 16: Vision Loss	Inclusion: Classroom Implications for the General and Special Educator	438
Chapter 17: Physical Disabilities and Health Disorders	Including Students with Physical Disabilities: Best Practices	464–465
Chapter 18: Gifted, Creative, and Talented	Academic Diversity: Differentiated Instruction	510–511
Chapter 18: Gifted, Creative, and Talented	Constructivist Teaching in Action: A High School Classroom Debate	512

IV. TEACHING IN ACTION EXERCISES FOR EACH VIDEO CASE

The following reflection exercises integrate concepts from the textbook and the Video Cases. Working with the Video Cases and the textbook together will greatly improve your understanding of this course's subject matter.

Reflection Questions for Chapter 1, "Understanding Exceptionality," and accompanying Video Case

Question 1.1

After reading Chapter 1 and watching the Video Case entitled "Teaching as a Profession: Collaboration with Colleagues," please answer the following questions:

a. How will you transfer what you know about being a collaborator to your teaching career? Where will you begin?

b. What are the benefits of expanding collaboration to include other service professionals such as health care professionals, psychologists, and social service professionals?

Reflection Questions for Chapter 2, "Education for All," and accompanying Video Cases

Question 2.1

After reading Chapter 2 and watching the Video Case entitled "Foundations: Meeting the Demands of Educational Legislation," please answer the following questions:

a. The current emphasis on standardized exams can contribute to a teacher's anxiety level. Some teachers feel that standardized exams fail to provide a complete description of a student's progress over time. Where do you stand on this issue?

b. In determining the least restrictive environment for a student with disabilities, what advice would you seek to help you in making such an important decision?

Question 2.2

After reading Chapter 2 and watching the Video Case entitled "Students with Special Needs: The Referral and Evaluation Process," please answer the following questions:

a. What questions have been raised for you about the legitimacy of the four phases of the referral process and what are the strengths of this process?

b. During the pre-referral process, what are some ways that you and the child-study team can collaborate to modify or adapt the current instruction?

Question 2.3

After reading Chapter 2 and watching the Video Case entitled "Teacher Accountability: A Student Teacher's Perspective," please answer the following questions:

a. What does it mean to you personally to be a highly qualified teacher?

b. Describe any concerns you face regarding teacher accountability, and what steps you can take to feel confident as a teacher regarding accountability.

Reflection Questions for Chapter 3, "Inclusion and Multidisciplinary Collaboration in the Early Childhood and Elementary School Years," and accompanying Video Cases

Question 3.1

After reading Chapter 3 and watching the Video Case entitled "Inclusion: Classroom Implications for the General and Special Educator," please answer the following questions:

a. What are the advantages for students who have IEPs? What challenges do IEPs pose for teachers and specialists?

b. How does the partnership between the general and special education teachers benefit students with a varying range of abilities and disabilities?

Question 3.2 ....

After reading Chapter 3 and watching the Video Case entitled "Inclusion: Grouping Strategies for Inclusive Classrooms," please answer the following questions:

a. What do you see as the most important considerations to successfully grouping students?

b. How can you deliver instruction in ways that foster the individual learning styles of all students?

Reflection Questions for Chapter 4, "Transition and Adult Life," and accompanying Video Case

Question 4.1 ....

After reading Chapter 4 and watching the Video Case entitled "Developing Student Self-Esteem: Peer Editing Process," please answer the following questions:

a. A student named Fritz talks about how constructive criticism helps him succeed in school. Success in school leads to feeling successful in life, he maintains. How does this process foster the development of self-determination in students?

b. What implications does the development of self-esteem have on the academic success of students with disabilities?

Reflection Questions for Chapter 5, "Multicultural and Diversity Issues," and accompanying Video Cases

Question 5.1 ....

After reading Chapter 5 and watching the Video Case entitled "Diversity: Teaching in a Multiethnic Classroom," please answer the following questions:

a. How does the lesson in the video support the concept of multicultural education?

b. What are the benefits for students who are provided experiences about a variety of cultures?

After reading Chapter 5 and watching the Video Case entitled "Culturally Responsive Teaching: A Multicultural Lesson for Elementary Students" please answer the following questions:

  a. If you were to begin teaching tomorrow and your goal was to teach using a multicultural perspective, how would you go about it? Explain your idea.

  b. In this video, Dr. Francis advises new teachers to become responsive multicultural educators by learning everything they can about countries around the world. You have probably had the experiences of studying particular countries. How has the experience broadened your world-view?

Question 5.3..

After reading Chapter 5 and watching the Video Case entitled "Bilingual Education: An Elementary Two-Way Immersion Program," please answer the following questions:

  a. The two teachers in this video segment work together closely to teach students in two different languages. What do you see as the strengths of the two-way bilingual method? What are some of the weaknesses of this approach?

  b. What do you think of the public debate over bilingual education? How does this video segment either challenge or support your views?

Reflection Questions for Chapter 6, "Exceptionality and the Family," and accompanying Video Cases

Question 6.1..

After reading Chapter 6 and watching the Video Case entitled "Home-School Communication: The Parent-Teacher Conference," please answer the following questions:

  a. In what ways does effective home-school communication help teachers gain sensitivity to the individual needs of each family?

  b. In this video segment, how does Jim diffuse a potentially difficult discussion with the parent of one of his students? How will you approach a parent who displays anxiety about his or her child's performance when you become a teacher?

Question 6.2..

After reading Chapter 6 and watching the Video Case entitled "Communicating with Parents: Tips and Strategies for Future Teachers," please answer the following questions:

a. In this video segment, a father describes his hunger for the details of his child's day so he can be an effective parent. In your opinion, how can sharing insights about a child's experiences in the classroom help create a synergy between home and school?

b. In what ways is a teacher's role in communicating with parents affected when a student has disabilities?

Reflection Questions for Chapter 7, "Learning Disabilities," and accompanying Video Cases

Question 7.1..

After reading Chapter 7 and watching the Video Case entitled "Elementary Reading Instruction: A Balanced Literacy Program," please answer the following questions:

a. The text states that children with learning difficulties often have considerable difficulties in becoming proficient readers. What steps can a teacher take to ensure that a literacy program is appropriate for students with learning disabilities?

b. Establishing a balanced literacy program can take a good deal of time. What do you see as the benefits of laying a foundation over a long period of time? What might the disadvantages be?

Question 7.2..

After reading Chapter 7 and watching the Video Case entitled "Inclusion: Classroom Implications for the General and Special Educator," please answer the following questions:

a. Considering the wide range of student abilities, when and why is it important for new teachers to seek the support of other teachers?

b. What steps can the general education and special education teachers take in planning successful inclusion programs that effectively promote academic support, motivation among students, and the development of social-emotional skills for students with learning disabilities?

Question 8.1

After reading Chapter 8 and watching the Video Case entitled "Including
Students with High Incidence Disabilities: Strategies for Success,"
please answer the following questions:

    a. Children with ADHD often benefit from extra help and carefully
structured learning tasks. What can you do now to prepare for
teaching children with ADHD?

    b. What strategies will you employ as a teacher to help students
with ADHD improve their self-management skills?

Question 8.2

After reading Chapter 8 and watching the Video Case entitled
"Classroom Management: Best Practices," please answer the
following questions:

    a. How can you structure your classroom to enhance the learning
of students with ADHD?

    b. Describe specific techniques you will utilize to modify academic
instructions to support learners with ADHD. Describe why you
feel these techniques will benefit your students.

Question 8.3

After reading Chapter 8 and watching the Video Case entitled
"Metacognition: Helping Students Become Strategic Learners," please
answer the following questions:

    a. One strategy demonstrated in this Video Case is marking up
the text. What do see as the benefits of this strategy for
students with ADHD?

    b. Cognitive challenges can continue into adolescence and
adulthood for individuals with ADHD. In what ways does it
serve adolescents with ADHD to learn about how they think?

Question 9.1

After reading Chapter 9 and watching the Video Case entitled "Classroom Management: Handling a Student with Behavior Problems," please answer the following questions:

a. What behavioral expectations do you feel will be important to establish in your classroom? How will clearly defining these expectations assist you in addressing the challenging behaviors of students with emotional and/or behavioral disorders?

b. What types of behavioral issues do you think will challenge you when you begin teaching? What types of interventions will you use to address these behaviors?

Question 9.2

After reading Chapter 9 and watching the Video Case entitled "Elementary Classroom Management: Basic Strategies," please answer the following questions:

a. In this Video Case, you saw teachers use techniques such as children's literature and role-play for encouraging positive social behavior. Do you feel that these are effective methods of teaching pro-social behavior? If not, what are some other ways you would teach appropriate social behaviors to your students?

b. How can you help students transfer positive behaviors that occur in the classroom to other school environments such as the playground, the hallways, and the lunchroom?

Question 9.3

After reading Chapter 9 and watching the Video Case entitled "Social and Emotional Development: Understanding Adolescents," please answer the following questions:

a. In this Video Case, you saw the guidance counselor lead a small group discussion about effective strategies to help control anger in everyday life. What do you think of the way the students were encouraged to devise strategies that will work for them?

b. Why is it important for teachers to listen to their students? How can you show your students that you value their feelings?

Reflection Questions for Chapter 10, "Intellectual Disabilities," and accompanying Video Cases

Question 10.1

After reading Chapter 10 and watching the Video Case entitled "Assistive Technology in the Inclusive Classroom: Best Practices," please answer the following questions:

a. In what ways do you see assistive technology making inclusion possible for some students with intellectual disabilities? What challenges are teachers faced with when a student in their classroom relies on assistive technology devices?

b. In this Video Case, you see an aid helping the student using assistive technology. What do you see as the benefits of a student having an aid? Do you have any concerns about having an aid in your classroom?

Question 10.2

After reading Chapter 10 and watching the Video Case entitled "Inclusion: Grouping Strategies for Inclusive Classrooms," please answer the following questions:

a. How will learning styles and diverse academic levels affect the way you will structure small groups in an inclusive classroom?

b. What did you notice about the collaboration that took place between the students with individual needs and typical learners? How would you characterize these interactions?

Reflection Questions for Chapter 11, "Communication Disorders," and accompanying Video Case

Question 11.1

After reading Chapter 11 and watching the Video Case entitled "Assistive Technology in the Inclusive Classroom: Best Practices," please answer the following questions:

a. If you have a student with a communication disorder in your classroom using an assistive technology device as a primary method of communicating in the classroom, in what ways can you prepare typical learners to demonstrate respect for this student? How can you encourage typical learners to include a child with communication disorders in their activities?

b. In what ways will assistive technology aid or hinder your ability to make the general curriculum available for all students in your classroom?

Reflection Questions for Chapter 12, "Severe and Multiple Disabilities," and accompanying Video Case

Question 12.1

After reading Chapter 12 and watching the Video Case entitled "Foundations: Meeting the Demands of Educational Legislation," please answer the following questions:

a. What are your personal views and opinions on including students with severe and multiple disabilities in the accountability system? How can you ensure that assessments are appropriate for these students?

b. What are some alternatives to standardized testing that can ensure that schools are held to high standards of learning for students with severe and multiple disabilities?

Reflection Questions for Chapter 13, "Autism Spectrum Disorder," and accompanying Video Cases

Question 13.1

After reading Chapter 13 and watching the Video Case entitled "Including Students with High Incidence Disabilities: Strategies for Success," please answer the following questions:

a. In what ways can the strategies that were employed in this Video Case help you meet the IEP goals for students with autism spectrum disorders?

b. In what ways do you foresee students with Autism Spectrum Disorders requiring extra support in the classroom?

After reading Chapter 13 and watching the Video Case entitled "Classroom Management: Best Practices," please answer the following questions:

    a. How can you utilize the principals of behaviorism to develop effective classroom management strategies for students with autism spectrum disorders?

    b. What prior experiences have you had to prepare for teaching students with autism spectrum disorders?

Reflection Questions for Chapter 14, "Traumatic and Acquired Brain Injury," and accompanying Video Case

Question 14.1 ....

After reading Chapter 14 and watching the Video Case entitled "Classroom Management: Best Practices," please answer the following questions:

    a. As a teacher, how might you benefit from collaboration with medical personnel when deciding upon effective management strategies for students who have suffered from traumatic brain injuries?

    b. Why is it important for teachers to have knowledge about how a traumatic brain injury can affect a student's behavior? How can this knowledge help you in selecting the most appropriate classroom management strategies?

Reflection Questions for Chapter 15, "Hearing Loss," and accompanying Video Cases

Question 15.1 ....

After reading Chapter 15 and watching the Video Case entitled "Teaching Technology Skills: An Elementary School Lesson on PowerPoint," please answer the following questions:

    a. How can technology such as PowerPoint be useful for students with hearing loss? What challenges can the use of technology in the classroom present for teachers?

    b. Do you feel that technology helps students with a hearing loss access the general curriculum? If so, in what ways?

Reflection Questions for Chapter 16, "Vision Loss," and accompanying Video Case

Question 16.1 ....

After reading Chapter 16 and watching the Video Case entitled "Inclusion: Classroom Implications for the General and Special Educator," please answer the following questions:

   a. How can collaboration between the general and special education teachers benefit students with vision loss in inclusive educational settings?

   b. Do you feel that an inclusive setting is appropriate for students with severe vision loss? What types of extra support might these students require?

Reflection Questions for Chapter 17, "Physical Disabilities and Health Disorders," and accompanying Video Case

Question 17.1 ....

After reading Chapter 17 and watching the Video Case entitled "Including Students with Physical Disabilities: Best Practices," please answer the following questions:

   a. In this Video Case, Lisa Kelleher describes her role as a teacher in an inclusive classroom as being quite multifaceted. Are there any aspects of her role that surprised you or made you envision your future role as a teacher differently? Explain.

   b. What skills does the elementary classroom aid bring to her work with the student in the video who has spina bifida? How does the aid take the student's academic and social/emotional development into account when planning activities?

Reflection Questions for Chapter 18, "Gifted, Creative, and Talented," and accompanying Video Cases

Question 18.1 ....

After reading Chapter 18 and watching the Video Case entitled "Academic Diversity: Differentiated Instruction," please answer the following questions:

   a. Why is it important to consider students' strengths during instructional planning? How can you ensure that all students will be provided with appropriate challenges?

b. What specific considerations need to be made when teaching gifted, creative, and talented students?

Question 18.2..

After reading Chapter 18 and watching the Video Case entitled "Constructivist Teaching in Action: A High School Classroom Debate," please answer the following questions:

a. Do you feel that utilizing a constructivist learning philosophy can help gifted, creative, and talented students maximize learning? Explain.

b. The text states that designing and implementing curricula for students who are gifted presents significant but rewarding challenges. Do you feel that a constructivist learning approach can help you become a more flexible and creative teacher?

VIEWING ASSESSMENT GUIDE FOR VIDEO CASES

Students and professors can use this viewing rubric to gauge understanding of the Video Case. Use this page as you prepare your in-class exercises or homework assignments.

Name: _____

Chapter: _____

Video Case Title: _____

Questions for the Student:

   a. Describe the main issues, problems, or strategies depicted in this case. Which of these, in your opinion, is the most important aspect of the case?

     _____

     _____

     _____

     _____

     _____

   b. What are the teacher's key actions in this case? (i.e., his/her skills, approaches, activities, behaviors)

     _____

     _____

     _____

     _____

     _____

   c. How do the key issues within this case relate to the topic(s) discussed in this chapter?

     _____

     _____

_____

_____

_____

_____

d. Reflect upon your own classroom experiences with this topic. Have you had, as either a student or a teacher, any experiences that are similar to those portrayed within the Video Case? In what ways were they similar or different?

_____

_____

_____

_____

_____

_____

e. As a teacher, how would you handle the situations that were presented in the case?

_____

_____

_____

_____

_____

_____

f. How has this Video Case influenced or shaped your view of teaching and learning?

_____

_____

_____

_____

_____

CONNECTIONS BETWEEN HM VIDEO CASES AND THE PRAXIS II TEACHER PREPARATION EXAM

Houghton Mifflin's Video Cases in Education *can also help you master important content that will be included on the Praxis II Teacher Preparation Exam. Viewing these cases will help reinforce key concepts that will be covered within the exam questions. The chart below lists the various sections of the exam and the specific Video Cases that relate to each section.*

Section of PRAXIS II Exam	Correlating HM Video Cases
Section I: STUDENTS AS LEARNERS This section of the exam covers developmental issues, special education, multicultural education, bilingual education, diverse learning styles, motivation, and classroom management.	**CASES ON DIVERSITY AND MULTICULTURAL EDUCATION** • Diversity: Teaching in a Multiethnic Classroom • Bilingual Education: An Elementary Two-Way Immersion Program • Culturally Responsive Teaching: A Multicultural Lesson for Elementary Students • Multiple Intelligences: Elementary School Instruction • Gender Equity in the Classroom: Girls and Science **CASES ON DEVELOPMENTAL ISSUES** • Developing Student Self-Esteem: Peer Editing Process • Social and Emotional Development: The Influence of Peer Groups • Social and Emotional Development: Understanding Adolescents **CASES ON COGNITIVE DEVELOPMENT AND MOTIVATION** • Constructivist Teaching in Action: A High School Classroom Debate • Metacognition: Helping Students Become Strategic Learners • Motivating Adolescent Learners: Curriculum Based on Real Life • Modeling: Social Cognitive Theory in a High School Chemistry Lesson • Vygotsky's Zone of Proximal Development: Increasing Cognition in an Elementary Literacy Lesson

Section of PRAXIS II Exam	Correlating HM Video Cases
Section I: STUDENTS AS LEARNERS (continued)	**CASES ON SPECIAL EDUCATION** • Inclusion: Grouping Strategies for Inclusive Classrooms • Inclusion: Classroom Implications for the General and Special Educator • Academic Diversity: Differentiated Instruction • Foundations: Aligning Instruction with Federal Legislation **CASES ON CLASSROOM MANAGEMENT** • Classroom Management: Best Practices • Classroom Management: Handling a Student with Behavior Problems • Elementary Classroom Management: Basic Strategies • Secondary Classroom Management: Basic Strategies
Section II: INSTRUCTION AND ASSESSMENT This section of the exam covers cognitive processes associated with student learning, instructional planning, lesson planning, and assessment techniques.	**CASES ON INSTRUCTIONAL STRATEGIES** • Elementary School Language Arts: Inquiry Learning • Middle School Science Instruction: Inquiry Learning • Cooperative Learning in the Elementary Grades: Jigsaw Model • Cooperative Learning: High School History Lesson • Inclusion: Grouping Strategies for Inclusive Classrooms • Elementary Reading Instruction: A Balanced Literacy Program • Middle School Reading Instruction: Integrating Technology • Elementary Writing Instruction: Process Writing • An Expanded Definition of Literacy: Meaningful Ways to Use Technology • Multimedia Literacy: Integrating Technology into the Middle School Curriculum • Reading in the Content Areas: An Interdisciplinary Unit on the 1920s • Motivating Adolescent Learners: Curriculum Based on Real Life • Academic Diversity: Differentiated Instruction

Section of PRAXIS II Exam	Correlating HM Video Cases
Section II: INSTRUCTION AND ASSESSMENT *(continued)*	• Constructivist Teaching in Action: A High School Classroom Debate • Modeling: Social Cognitive Theory in a High School Chemistry Lesson • Integrating Internet Research: High School Social Studies • Integrating Technology to Improve Student Learning: A High School Science Simulation • Using Technology to Promote Discovery Learning: A High School Geometry Lesson **CASES ON ASSESSMENT** • Assessment in the Elementary Grades: Formal and Informal Literacy Assessment • Assessment in the Middle Grades: Measurement of Student Learning • Portfolio Assessment: Elementary Classroom • Formative Assessment: High School History Class • Grading: Strategies and Approaches • Performance Assessment: Student Presentations in a High School English Class
Section III: COMMUNICATION TECHNIQUES This section of the exam covers verbal and nonverbal communication, interacting with students, cultural and gender differences that impact communication in the classroom, and questioning techniques.	**CASES ON QUESTIONING TECHNIQUES** • Elementary School Language Arts: Inquiry Learning • Using Technology to Promote Discovery Learning: A High School Geometry Lesson • Middle School Science Instruction: Inquiry Learning • Middle School Reading Instruction: Integrating Technology **CASES ON CULTURAL AND GENDER ISSUES** • Diversity: Teaching in a Multiethnic Classroom • Bilingual Education: An Elementary Two-Way Immersion Program • Culturally Responsive Teaching: A Multicultural Lesson for Elementary Students • Gender Equity in the Classroom: Girls and Science

Section of PRAXIS II Exam	Correlating HM Video Cases
Section III: COMMUNICATION TECHNIQUES *(continued)*	**CASES ON COMMUNICATION ISSUES WITH STUDENTS** • Classroom Management: Handling a Student with Behavior Problems • Elementary Classroom Management: Basic Strategies • Secondary Classroom Management: Basic Strategies • Classroom Management: Best Practices • Social and Emotional Development: Understanding Adolescents
Section IV: PROFESSION AND COMMUNITY This section of the exam covers professional development, best practices, becoming a reflective practitioner, communication with parents, education and the law.	**CASES ON PROFESSIONAL ISSUES** • Teaching as a Profession: Collaboration with Colleagues • Teaching as a Profession: What Defines Effective Teaching? • Teacher Accountability: A Student Teacher's Perspective **CASES ON LEGAL ISSUES** • Legal and Ethical Dimensions of Teaching: Reflections from Today's Educators • Foundations: Aligning Instruction with Federal Legislation **CASES ON COMMUNICATING WITH PARENTS** • Home-School Communication: The Parent-Teacher Conference • Parental Involvement in School Culture: A Literacy Project